BITE-SIZED
BOOKS

A Bite-Sized Business Book

Bid for Success

Building the Right Strategy and Team

Tim Emmett

Published by Bite-Sized Books Ltd 2015

The right of Tim Emmett to be identified as the author of this work has been asserted by him in accordance with the Copyright, Design and Patents Act 1988
ISBN: 9781521094235

For my two great supporters –
my mother, Mary, and my wife, Alicja.

Bite-Sized Books Ltd
Cleeve Croft, Cleeve Road, Goring RG8 9BJ UK
information@bite-sizedbooks.com
Registered in the UK. Company Registration No: 9395379

Contents

Introduction

This little book is not meant to be a definitive technical business text about bidding and tendering for contracts and services. Many worthy tomes exist written by greater experts on the whole business of constructing technical offers and financial models. This book does not purport to emulate them in any way.

This is a highly personal account of some of the key issues that all of us face when tackling a business competition organised through competitive tendering. It is not comprehensive, but it covers the top topics and more importantly it addresses the often neglected human dimension to the process both in terms of the client and, ironically, in terms of the bidders' own organisations. Often the most infuriating, frustrating aspect of bid or proposal preparation is dealing with one's own colleagues and piloting the proposal through to a successful conclusion.

This book looks at the key relationships that have to be in place internally, if there is to be any chance of external success. It also considers the team and the dynamics of making that team successful; it lays bare some of the politics and personality challenges that will be faced no matter what position you may hold in your organisation. It considers the tactics you may want to deploy to ensure your bid crosses all the internal lines before it even makes it through the client's door and hopefully, gives you some career guidance along the way.

Bidding is a stressful and expensive process and the burden often falls, ultimately, on one individual – you. This book will hopefully hearten you and not depress you, enlighten you and not make you frown, entertain you without being flippant and offer you some insights based on experience which you can add to your own personal catalogue to stand you in good stead as your career falters, develops or takes off – which I sincerely hope it will do.

Chapter 1
Markets, Money, Mortality (or, is it morality?)

You've read the introduction? If not, please do so because gentle reader (as the Victorians would put it) you will not be clear about what this Bite-Sized Book is not.

No market, no money

Chapter 1 is all about markets, money and your mortality in connection with both of these. Without a market, there is no money and without money there is no market and this is as applicable in the world of competitive bidding or tendering as it is in any other commercial activity.

So: you are fulfilling your company strategy in identifying potential opportunities for which you should prepare bids. Wrong. You first of all need to be clear about what your company or your organisation actually does or wants to do.

Furthermore, you need to know who else is doing it or wants to do it. This means a bit more than a morning in the company of Mr Google or Mrs Yahoo, helpful though they may be. You need to develop a high level pipeline of areas of interest and answers (often referred to as solutions) and opportunities that you or your company can provide. If you are already in an established market, this will be slightly easier than if you are planning to enter a new one or even more significantly, if you are trying to create a market where none has previously existed (a major challenge). For example, it may be necessary to create a commercial and political alliance to lobby and exert pressure to open up a market that has previously been the preserve of the public sector, for example in transport, healthcare, custodial services and education. All these sectors are of course political minefields, but true innovation and accountability is really only achieved when there is an open and transparent market that operates to the benefit of customers, rather than producers.

There are contrasting strategies for these and it will take more than a mouthful that this little book can provide to develop them in full – but here is more than a taste.

Knowing the unknowns

The main message has to be: focus on what you know, apply what you know to what you don't know and assess whether what you don't know is likely to be worth knowing. However, you also should be aware of your own mortality and work-life balance in all of this. As a specialist in whatever field, you will need to have advanced technical knowledge of your product or services or be able to access experts who do. You need to be talking to them continuously about what is happening in your markets or those markets you would like to be in. This means attending conferences and workshops which could be international, reading the trade press of your chosen industry and following news items that will give you clues about new opportunities and the timing of them happening. A cardinal rule to remember is that once an opportunity is in the public domain, it is often too late to mount a bid. To be a successful bidder requires advanced market information: you need to know before others do and then you can get some serious competitive advantage that will help you to win. Waiting to respond to a Request For Proposal, Invitation To Tender or Invitation To Negotiate means that you will be too late and you will lose. Ah yes – those magic words that dog your life as a bidder and that are frequently abbreviated. Get used to them right now. These terms are the client's shopping list and define the process about how they want to buy goods and services. The arrival of one of these in your in-box is always guaranteed to turn your stomach over, because at this point you are truly under starter's orders and the race has begun.

Don't be excluded

Because you understand your industry, you should know what's going on and this means you may be able to influence the shape of the clients' requirements. Sometimes clients assist in this by organising soft market testing, where they select players in the industry and consult them about the type of job they want doing and to garner your ideas on the best options for doing it. This is good news and you should try and get involved in any kind of early dialogue. It sounds like common sense, but you would be surprised at how many organisations miss out. In the public and private sectors, the big four global consultancy companies are very adept and adroit at getting advanced knowledge of what is going on and also at excluding others from the process. The international boutiques are also extremely adept at keeping the Big Four at bay, so it could be tough. You must ensure that you are not excluded through building relationships.

If you are working in a smaller organisation the stakes will be much higher because your time and therefore your focus is more precious, so invest time wisely. All clients believe in markets and competition, allegedly, but sometimes the reality is far from this and they prefer to work with a concert party of favoured buddies with every intention of excluding you. This is bad news until you get to be one of them, by which time you will want to exclude those at the bottom of the ladder, whilst loudly espousing the virtues and merits of the free market and the benefits of competition from your lofty position at the top. At which point, beware hubris: staying at the top can be more difficult than getting there.

It's not fair

Understanding the dynamics of your market is therefore an important starting point and if you or your boss feel that it is tilted in any way against you, you need a strategy to address this, possibly involving your board and maybe a journalist or two. An arch exponent in this arena is Richard Branson, notably in the area of big ticket contracts. He has been unafraid to challenge client authority; he has sought judicial reviews of tendering processes; hired m'learned friends at great expense, briefed the media and has won through in the end. From being an outsider, he has become an insider and one to be feared. You should not be backward in coming forward and never accept any comments from the client about "better luck next time", or "now you have more experience it will stand you in good stead for next time." Or, "sour grapes; they lost".

There never is a next time; there is only the here and now and you need to win. However, such challenges are often perceived to be high risk and expensive. "Better not to rock the boat", or to get a reputation for being "vexatious" or a nuisance. I would counsel against this strategy, counterintuitive though it might seem. Do not imagine for one moment that any market playing field anywhere on Planet Earth is entirely level. The important part is understanding this, not necessarily accepting it and then choosing your battleground carefully and deciding after measured analysis whether it is worth bidding.

If you perceive genuine market challenges that appear insuperable, you have a stark choice – either take them on or walk away. Some great innovators have taken on entrenched and biased markets and been successful: Richard Branson, and James Dyson; UK companies such as Capita and CfBT Education Trust have all had to break open markets to establish themselves and become successful.

You may also be told that to gain access to a new market, you should partner with an existing player or market incumbent as a subcontractor, become part of a consortium and win your spurs that way. It is true that most projects require a package of skills and experience not all of which may be present in one bidding organisation. If you are new to a market, this may be the only way to get access to it. The other way to look at it is to assemble your own consortium and present the case for a powerful new player to enter the market.

In the UK and elsewhere in the West, we like to believe our own publicity that our markets are transparent, open, well managed and regulated and that the further east or south you travel the more bent and opaque markets become. Poppycock. All markets have biases, barriers to entry and corruption of both an overt and covert nature is ever present, in spite of laws designed to prevent its more obvious manifestations.

You need to keep on the straight and narrow, but do not be afraid to use a big stick. If you believe or, even better, can prove that you have suffered an injustice, do not be afraid to complain and to seek restitution. Public sector clients get very nervous about this, and counter-intuitively, for that reason you may not be penalised. If you keep your head down, you will generally be ignored and regarded as unimportant. Make your arguments rationally and evenly and you may be surprised how much progress you can make.

If you are bidding into a major multilateral agency, for example the EU or ADB, you will be ignored anyway and appealing decisions will not make any difference at all. However, you should be wary of these outfits in the first place, because you will not make any major EBITDA through contracts with them.

Knowing the knowns

After your market analysis, which includes talking with other competitors and joining trade organisations, you will need a business development budget which need not be large, but which needs to be targeted, so you can travel overseas or nationally, depending on where the opportunity resides. This will be essential. The best bids on any topic always reveal an understanding of the ultimate purpose of the client requirement and show a level of detail and knowledge that can only come from visits, interviews, geography and maybe some interviews with potential beneficiaries. This means you must be thorough in your research and offer insights that augment what the client is seeking, showing how engaged you are in proposing a solution.

Once you have walked the course, and prior to the release of any official documentation, you should be in a strong position to convince your colleagues that this is an opportunity to bid for and to win. You and your company will be known in the sector; you will have been able to reveal your knowledge and expertise to the client, informally and above all you will have made the effort to engage with the requirement over and above information that will be publicly available; you will have gained some idea of budgets and you will now know what is important to the client and what they want to achieve.

You are now a market expert, an in-company guru and of course completely convinced that the project is viable and winnable. You have to be convinced about this, because if you are not convinced, do not expect anyone else to be and if you bid, without this mind set you will lose. And this is all about winning.

Chapter 2

Bring Solutions: Answering the Exam Questions

What is this all about?

We've done our market analysis; we've enlisted the support and active participation of our bosses; we think we can make some money; so what are we actually going to do?

Imagine an ITT or RFP is an examination, one of the old sort where you can take books and stuff into the exam hall, or prepare the answers in advance, but where sometimes all the subsidiary information can overwhelm you: too much information, in other words. You need to stand back and give the whole requirement the benefit of your clear thinking and astute insights.

Doing this alone can be a challenge, so you should assemble your core bid team, unless it is just you, and arrange a kick-off informal workshop to ask the overriding question that you should repeat periodically during the process: "What does the client want and are we fulfilling that need?

To bid, or not to bid

The object of bidding is to win, not to make up the numbers. Bidding is a very expensive operation for all trading businesses, it can also be their lifeblood; not bidding enables a corporate sigh of relief because of the avoided effort and sometimes a misguided understanding of "opportunity cost", that is think of all the other stuff we could/should be doing, instead of this, or wow, that was a close shave!

There are also occasions, particularly in larger companies, where being seen to bid is important. I am sceptical about this. Coming second or third on major bids just for the sake of visibility is a high price to pay, especially if you are leading your company's bid.

Advice under these circumstances: find another job. You are too good to be treated that way.

Back to the exam question. What is it that the client is looking for? What does your company have to design for them that will enable you to be the preferred bidder?

Typically a bid is evaluated according to two main criteria – technical and financial, with the technical offer being of sufficient quality before the financial offer is taken into consideration. This enables all clients to say that they have purchased the optimal solution or product at the most "economically advantageous" price. This of course means the cheapest deal, not necessarily the best value. Remember, procurement is an industry; lots of people make a healthy living out of designing systems and processes that appear transparent but in reality are opaque and of course require constant re-engineering. If you want a new anorak, join the Chartered Institute of Purchasing and Supply. The professional associations always enable producer interest to survive and thrive; you may become a member of one of them and perhaps follow a diploma course. This would help you to make the transition from supplier to buyer at some point downstream in your career, if you arrive at a point where you believe such treachery is necessary.

Avoid camel design

There are a number of ways of designing a solution for a bid and this book is too short and interesting to address all of them. Assembling the right people is obviously a starting point, but your core solution design team should not be too big, otherwise you will end up designing a camel that no-one can ride in an environment where camels do not thrive. So the basic design framework becomes very important as does the work plan into which it fits and of which you are indisputably in charge. You, as bite-sized bidder, must own the timeframe and it becomes the discipline that drives the whole bid along.

Designing a bid solution is a bit like laying a carpet: once you start putting it on the floor, changing your mind about the pattern and ripping it up is costly and consumes valuable time. Make this clear at the outset. So investing time in agreeing a limited range of solutions or answers to the client requirements is well worth while. Ask yourself and your team what the customer is really looking for; what kind of people, materials or equipment will be necessary; how can we relay trust reliability and integrity through what we do; what is project scope, that is what are the limitations of our offer for the price being considered?

The EBITDA boys and girls will be right onto this latter point.

Globally, the client trend is towards more for less. Value added has to be hard wired in, so don't kid yourself that you'll get extra for it. The RFP will usually guide you through the exam questions; if by any chance it does not and you have a freer rein, set our own headings and give yourself page limits for text and diagrams. Time limit yourself and others in writing responses, just as you would in a formal examination. Data and statistics are always useful, provided they are relevant and above all, digestible. Draw on experience and examples to give your solution life and vitality. Guide your reader with interesting subheadings; keep the paragraphs short and inject some spontaneity into your writing. Increasingly, through the magic of on-line tendering, these limits are helpfully set by the clients, but it is good bid discipline to do it yourself.

What really puts people off bids is the vast amount of writing that is often required and in the bite sized universe of social media and digital technology, people are less and less good at writing sustained pieces of text that are clear, jargon-free and easy to read. However, there is still a client expectation that this can be done. Do not believe that PowerPoint and bullet points are in any way a substitute for a tightly written piece of prose, useful at times though they may be.

As you map out your offer, allocate tasks to your specialists and be clear what you want from them, not what they would like to offer. Set out the key questions and develop a rapid response to them, using flip charts or on screen. As soon as you have a framework in place, you and your colleagues will begin to feel more confident and the bid preparation will gather momentum. Make notes of great examples and how they are relevant to the client requirement and how you would apply your experience in a way that is distinctive and makes a quantifiable difference together with some performance indicators and measures.

As you identify the deadlines for inputs, be aware that they will all be broken and that the final edit will be down to you. Build in masses of contingency.

When getting the solution answers under way, you need to get your boss on side, because he or she will always have the best ideas, whilst yours will always not be quite as good. Make it a broad church and get them on board; suggest that the boss should pen the executive summary – you can always doctor it later – this way you get the benefit of their thinking right up front and they of course appear on page one, which is where they should be, or think they should be.

As the owner of the bid, you need the highest understanding of what the client wants and how to angle the answers to the questions.

Bid processes

Some bid processes require a high degree of interaction with the client; these may be termed negotiated processes, or more thrillingly, competitive dialogues, or a variation on this. What this means is that you and your bid team get to meet the client through a series of structured, or sometimes unstructured, meetings where you introduce your team and address specific requirements, often through prepared papers and presentations, all of which lead to something called a BAFO, or a best and final offer. The idea is that after all this dialogue and discussion, your offer is so finely tuned and honed that the evaluation against other bidders becomes much easier. All of you are capable of doing the job, so what will the difference be? The answer will be price. All the bidders will have passed the quality threshold, so it is just a matter of money – and don't believe anything else you are told when the debrief comes as to why you lost.

Notwithstanding the cash, winning through a competitive dialogue requires stamina, attention to detail and a really high level of concentration. You also have the opportunity to study the client team carefully. A good exercise in solution design is to do some deep due diligence on the people you meet and those who will evaluate your bid. What do you know about them? What do you need to know about them?

For example, are the men on the team blokey blokes, regular dudes, who like football, golf and cool holiday destinations? Or are they straight shooters who go to Sunday school? Watch out for the techies and extreme personality types. Are the women hard-nosed, competitive women in a man's world or relaxed, capable individuals? How do the women and the men interact on the panel; who is in the driving seat? And, inevitably on major bids, who are the hired consultants on the panel? They can be a real pain, because they serve two masters, the client and their employer, or if they are independent, they are looking to continue their assignment. Clients can also develop an unhealthy dependency on them and of course they add cost to the process which can affect your budget: money spent on them is not there to be spent on you.

These type of bids add substantial cost for you and keeping track of all the documents and iterations can be daunting and you will find that you may need an assistant to keep score – another bid cost. Making sure your team performs well and is polite and clear during the process is a key role for you. Being aggressive and impatient because of the onerous process will impede your solution development and irritate your client, who will also be feeling the strain and the pressure of multiple meetings with up to six different bid teams.

So let's talk about our team and how to get the best out of it.

Chapter 3
Lead the Team, live the Dream: Managing the Bid

The situation

You have scoped out the market; you have cosied up to the client; you can smell the sell: you are cooking on gas! Time to get your team together, because no-one can do a bid on their own and indeed it is very dangerous to do so, because you need "buy-in" from your busy colleagues, your boss and often your board (which in a small business could be your wife/husband/partner/family). And when it comes to bidding for a business opportunity, believe me, all your colleagues are very, very, busy doing other stuff that is miles more important than securing the next deal or contract and the future of the company and indeed their place on the payroll.

Why is this? Because bidding is seriously hard work, requiring long hours beyond the call of duty, lots of stress and deadlines and endless arguments or constructive discussions about the answer to the client's exam questions and then the constant nagging fear of the consequences of losing the work to a competitor and what that means for the company and in particular what it means for your career and in particular your boss' career. Which of course is on a different trajectory from yours.

Authority: have you got the juice?

So you and your boss (Steve, Darren, Kylie, Elvis) need to spend some quality face time together to discuss the bid team and your leadership of it, because you need that stuff called "authority" to make it happen. You may have a natural authority, which is helpful in the world of bidding because it means you won't put up with any nonsense, but others have authority too and in a bid process your authority will need to trump theirs if you and the bid are to be successful. You need to get the flow through authority from your boss for the entire process. If he or she leaves or gets fired along the way, you will need the buy in from your boss's boss – always a good move in any case, and what better than a bid to get that high visibility in the organisation. Remember your boss is more expensive than you – more expensive than you think he or she is and certainly more expensive than he or she deserves to be. You may also need to prepare a paper for the inevitable board meeting that summarises the opportunity, presents the indicative financial returns and the rationale for the whole enterprise.

Remember, you need all this high level juice – they are part of the team as well and will want to share in the glory of your success and probably deprive you of it into the bargain; and if the bid loses, well it was a long shot any way and the business development guy running the bid, well he or she didn't do a very good job and we now need to reduce the headcount…

You can complete the story yourself.

If possible, accompany your boss to the board; be passionate about the opportunity, focus on the returns, the prestige, the benefits and show them some sexy numbers. On a crowded agenda and if you have done your research right and had some preliminary conversations, you may be surprised at what you can achieve, because we're a team. You may also get some additional juice from a board member who can help you out and you need all the help you can get. Keeping your boss and the board updated is an important role for the bite-sized bidder, so ensure you come up with a quick and effective method of doing so. For example, pander to their specialist skills and knowledge, grease up to them on their favourite sports or interests (well, those you care to raise); complement them on their past or current achievements, new wives or cars. You can offer to circulate a regular, very short, briefing to board members; ask them if they have any client-side contacts; challenge them to be helpful to you in your corporate endeavour that will create value, not to mention a hefty dollop of EBITDA.

Team building

Boss approval, board approval and now sell the dream and build the team (did I just write that?)

You may well need partners, who will also have to go through this internal process as well, so they need time, which is in short supply to get their approvals, so they also need to read this book. On the internal front, at a minimum, you need financial expertise (well covered in a later chapter), specialist technical knowledge about the topic and the solution that the client is seeking, available experts who will do the work, either internal or external and some wizards who can do document preparation, who may include you. You also need a plan and a budget. If the bid requires substantial resourcing and the hiring of specialists such as lawyers to review contracts, or architects, you will need approval to spend.

And a word on the lawyers.

In a large company, there will be in-house lawyers, or counsel, as they often like to be called. These guys are always super busy, as well as super self-important and certainly won't have time for you and your irritating draft client contracts. The in-house guys will want to nickel and dime each clause and won't understand that most of it is non-negotiable at this stage and if you kick up a fuss you will probably be disqualified.

Managing lawyers, either in-house or externally appointed, is an art in itself. Remember, there are only two types of lawyer on planet Earth — those who enable deals to happen and those who obstruct deals from happening. You should want the former, but will frequently encounter the latter and you have to help them out. Typically this involves endless revision to documents with miles of tracked changes. If you can, and if your organisation is large enough, get your work delegated to a newish recruit to the lawyers with whom you can work and who may have yet to acquire the pomposity that can characterise the profession. Spend some time with the junior and get him or her to handle the in-house senior counsel and help them to shine in front of the boss. And when the bid has been submitted, don't forget to send a thank you note to the senior lawyer, thanking him for his help and complimenting the work of the junior as effusively as you can muster without vomiting.

Rather than start a war prematurely with the client, it is better to ask your in-house lawyers, with the utmost deference, to offer a commentary on the contract such that you can raise issues with the client, without being unduly adversarial.

In addition to draft contracts, there may be a requirement for a bid bond, if the contract is sufficiently large. A bid bond is a legal and financial instrument that equates to a percentage of the contract price and which has to be issued by a bank, backed by your company's money, and which can be used as leverage in negotiations. For example, if you walked away from the deal, the client may have the right to cash in the bond and take your money. Often, if you are successful, a bid bond gets converted to a performance bond, against which penalties can be charged if you do not deliver to expectations. All of this winds up the lawyers something rotten. And they will wind you up as a consequence.

However, there is nothing better on a bid team than the in-house counsel appointing and then managing their mates or buddies from an external firm. Hours of endless entertainment will ensue as the meter ticks and you see the win just slipping away and the bid in meltdown.

Managing the lawyers is a vital part of the teamwork and you should include them in all discussions as you do the finance people. They have the power to scupper your bid through the time old process of risk analysis.

Being lawyers, it will all be downside. You need to become a bit of a risk analyst yourself. The key question to ask is always, how likely is this to happen on a sliding scale from 10 to zero? If there is a high risk of clients delaying payment, for example, you should factor any of those costs into your financial proposal. The main risk is usually around technology and people – a failure in the former and human error in the latter. These risks can be mitigated by first of all being recognised and then addressed. Spell out the technology you use and how it should interface with what the client wants; spell out your approach to hiring and vetting staff and how you will performance manage them.

Plans and plans

It is your leadership and motivation that must galvanise the team and to do that you need to be organised with, you've guessed it, a plan. The plan will give the team confidence that you know what you're doing and more to the point will show them what they are supposed to be doing. There are many ways of doing plans, but the real art is to give yourself time within the plan to predict and then rectify all that will go wrong – which it will. Work backwards from the submission deadline, increasingly this will be via some kind of e-portal that will malfunction on submission day, and give yourself and your boss time to review and for Elvis or Kylie to "sign off".

This latter process is a key part of being a boss and also a key part of you keeping your job. At the point of sign-off, your boss is likely to be a) on holiday b) at a senior leadership away day in a place with no telecoms reception of any kind c) at his kids' school concert with his infinitely more difficult second wife d) reading a bedtime story – same situation as c) above. Learning point: find out and confirm availability and if it changes, which it will, ensure that you have some kind of authority in advance to sign off and despatch the bid.

In the plan set the deadlines by which you wish to receive inputs and then be merciless in chasing them because what you need asap is a draft, working document set out to your specification and that follows the client requirements in the RFP. Along the way, you will need some bid review deadlines so that you can walk through the responses identifying gaps and the inevitable quality issues ranging from content to grammar that will arise.

Clients generally want you to be creative and innovative, but then again, they don't, so you have to offer security with potential for innovation and new ways of delivering services or products that are affordable. Show the client that you have the capacity for innovation and that you have suggestions for how it can be achieved at no additional cost.

CVs and specialists

CVs of key staff will be a significant component of the bid, if it is for any kind of technical assistance or project management. The client may well ordain CV structure and layout. Observe this to the letter. You should also nominate a bid team member to take special responsibility for CVs and to develop a skill and knowledge in this area. Again, this could be you. Indeed it is a good skill for a bid manager to have, because you alone will have the total knowledge of how to finesse CVs against the specification, whether you are using your own colleagues or hiring in the expertise.

The specialists – and of course you may be one yourself – tend to like a lot of deference during the bid process; occasionally a specialist will want to hijack it and will behave like a prima donna (this will be in addition to your boss). The best tactic is to indulge the guru, but not to let him or her run off with the ball – this can lead to all kinds of trouble, not least your marginalisation in the bid that you are leading.

As a bite-sized bid leader, part of your skill is keeping the big beasts on side throughout the process. This may involve a bit of corporate hospitality and always make sure there are refreshments at bid meetings. You don't want a Top Gear situation emerging, for want of a decent sandwich or hot meal.

If you think making the dream work is going to be a challenge, fasten your seatbelts for a subsequent next chapter that concerns a couple of team members who only go by their initials – EBITDA and IRR. You won't meet them in person, but you will feel their presence like a poltergeist in a deluxe suburban residence.

Chapter 4
EBITDA and IRR

Who?

Now who in the hell are EBITDA and IRR and what difference do they make to the price of bananas and the world of the bite-sized bidder?

Well actually there's three of them, EBIT, DA and IRR, but DA is really a kind of Siamese twin to EBIT. IRR is the ever present gooseberry who likes to taunt them. They want to shake him or her off, but just can't do it.

What?

EBIT – earnings before interest and tax; DA – depreciation and amortisation. IRR – internal rate of return. As a bite sized bidder, you will hear a lot about these guys and their place in the galaxy of business development that you inhabit. They also inhabit other galaxies that you will only hear about and may even wonder whether they exist at all. Believe me, if they don't exist, they put up a sustained appearance of looking like they do. This is because they are the special friends, if not house trained pets, of accountants and the accountancy profession. So they need to be your friends too and could really help your career to blossom and for you to become an ace bidding professional, which is of course what you want to be and why you are reading this book.

How?

As you develop your bid, develop your proposal or hone your sale, you will also be working in lockstep with your business analyst or your company accountant. In certain circumstances, both of these could be good old you yourself. Chances are that even in a small organisation there will be some kind of financial expert who will work on the numbers and then proceed to rain extravagantly on your parade from a position of little market knowledge, but greater organisational superiority.

Now, it is really important to get the moneymen and women on side and I suggest you include them in all discussions from day one. That means before you even work out the solution that your potential customer is seeking. You also need to be able to impress them with your knowledge of accounting metrics and how EBITDA and IRR actually work.

Trap your finance guy for an informal chat along the lines of: "We're thinking of bidding for this great opportunity that will take us into new markets, elevate the position of the company and make serious money. Steve, Darren, Kylie, Elvis (or whoever your boss is) is really behind this". To which your financial friend (because he must be or become your friend, if you are in any way to be a successful bidder) will immediately ask about potential operating margin, gross margin, profit, contribution to overheads, net profit - but where he's really heading is into the arms of EBIT and DA.

Puppetry

Imagine EBIT and DA as two puppets controlled by the finance industry who put on regular shows for the rest of the finance industry – a bit like Punch and Judy. We all know the story but still can't resist watching it over and over again, maybe on a different beach with different company. It will never really have a digital equivalent, except perhaps on-line Japanese game shows involving the baiting of small, furry animals.

Loan interest and tax are an accountancy requirement even if you do not have loans or pay any tax. If you do have loans and tax to pay, they need to be acknowledged, if you don't it's kind of nice to think that you do and to acknowledge that you do. Make sense?

Then there is DA – depreciation and amortization. This includes money that is working capital for the business – daily cash requirement for example and of course the deprecation cost of all those assets you own. So these costs have to be accounted for, but only after the earnings on your contract have been counted. Remember accountancy is about counting – the clue is in the word itself. This is potentially good news because EBIT and DA will not be your global responsibility. So you need to make the number as hefty as possible, because while you may not have an abiding interest, I can assure that others will take a contrasting view.

Investors like to look at EBITDA as it gives them a false sense of security about the business, that is to say let's look at the good stuff before we have to service the bad stuff, that is actually pay interest and meet other liabilities.

EBITDA is a good metric for profitability but a lousy one for cash flow and remember your project will often require cash flow to get it going and to sustain it. Clients, no matter how positive their buying signals, can turn out to be very tardy payers. So the finance guys, who of course know this, will say great profitability but challenging cash flow, so don't bother. You will then have to persuade them that the client is good for the gold and that your sterling client relationship management will ensure prompt payment. The finance guys won't believe you, so it may be time to call Elvis….

The next act

So now we turn to another weapon in the bid armoury – IRR – the internal rate of return. This is where you can also shine in front of your financial colleagues. IRR is the here and now value of future cash returns from the deployment of capital on a project. It was always used for projects that required intensive hard infrastructure, for example hotels, hospitals and office blocks, but is now standard across all projects and programmes that require working capital investment as well. Given that clients are often reluctant to pay promptly, you and our finance colleagues will need some kind of grip on when an opportunity will break even and the cost of capital associated with this. The higher the IRR and the earlier you break even, the better the deal will look.

Many organisations spend a great deal of time on this calculation as a precursor to bidding and you as the bite sized bidder will need to enter these arguments in a spirited and intelligent way, even before you know what the solution looks like or what orders you are going to make. You will also find that should you win the work, corporate amnesia may well set in as the original finance guys may have left/been fired, you may have left/been fired, or the metrics will have changed anyway. The lesson here is, don't get hung up on this stuff, barrel on with your analysis, get your boss(es) on side and big up the numbers. Remember, you need internal competitive advantage long before you need it over other bidders and the client itself.

If you're a finance guy reading this and why shouldn't you be? You need to up your game in relation to your bidding colleagues. You should ensure that you get invited to team bid meetings, read the RFP documents, ask intelligent questions and above all engage with the topic and the industry within which you are working. It is not sufficient to warble on about being just a finance person or accountant, as though you could be in the fruit and veg business one day and bidding for premier league football broadcasting rights the next. Industry expertise is important; your experience in fruit and veg may be relevant and you should deploy your experience in a way that adds value rather than subtracting it; you should count up rather than count down and whilst rightly interrogating the EBITDA and IRR at an early stage, you should still be looking for reasons to support a bid rather than dismissing it too early. As a finance guy, you should also understand the competition and get excited about the opportunity and not diss your bidding colleagues in order to get the approval of your boss. Team work makes the dream work, as I believe another chapter in this book is entitled.

Reflective practice

If the bid team take the view that after examining all angles on the EBIT front, the opportunity should be disqualified, some reflections should be undertaken. If you find yourself competing internally on the EBITDA frontline, you may be in the right job but in the wrong company, or you may be in the wrong job in the right company. Either way, if it is a common occurrence it may be time to brush up your LinkedIn profile and get some new friends on Facebook.

So once you have agreed in principle acceptable metrics for EBITDA and IRR you can race ahead with the rest of the bid, keeping your financial friends close so that when the final financial model is presented for submission, there are no surprises. Aligning the technical proposal with the financial proposal is a key component of the bidding process and if you do not get this right, not only do you lose credibility in your organisation, you will lose credibility and confidence with your clients.

Chapter 5

Presentations: PowerPoint – the LowerPoint: Ensure that Technology Doesn't Destroy Value

So your financial proposal is agreed; your bid is submitted; and now you and the team have been invited, at very short notice to make a presentation as part of the highly technocratic evaluation process. So what do you do? Fire up the laptop and reach for the PowerPoint. Wrong.

From the day you have submitted the bid, you start to prepare for the presentation, after all you wouldn't be bidding, if you weren't good enough to win, would you? So, just when the team is exhausted get them together for a power talk before you touch the PowerPoint.

You are the bid leader, but when a presentation comes along a number of your gobby and opinionated colleagues, including potentially your boss or even the CEO will want to be in on the act, so early and detailed preparation is essential. You have already been managing your bid team, and only those who prepared the bid will really know what is in it. The presentation is an opportunity to develop your thinking about the product or service solution; to answer client questions and to move you into pole position to win the competition. You will be time limited and you need to ensure that all members of a potential presentation team – which may also be limited to a specific number of people or roles – know why they are there, why they are important and what difference they are going to make to the job.

It is a truism indeed to say that people buy from people, but they need to be the right people and someone has to be in charge. Running a presentation is not about a democracy. And if you are to be a great bid director or manager, that person has to be you and you will need to put a bit of stick about, because, let's face it, you have done most to of the work so far, and you don't want to hand it over to someone, inevitably more senior, who will have the potential to really cock it up.

Clients like to meet the boss, so prep Kylie or Darren well and in private. Bosses often think they are really good at presentations, but nine times out of ten, they need the most coaching, but of course never have the time to do it. Spend time with them and brief them thoroughly during which you will get the inevitable, "Why didn't you mention this, or do that or propose something else?" Persevere and be clear about the role of the boss in the presentation and seek his advice on who should be in the squad from which the team will be drawn. Keep it fluid at this stage. And get the boss to attend at least part of the preparation meeting. They all think they can walk in off a plane from the car park or board meeting and be pitch perfect. Believe me I've never met one of these. There are also those bosses who you should not be let_out in public at any time, ever. They are often founders or owners – be very careful about fielding them at all times.

The squad is in the room, you are in charge, and no-one bar a very few have actually read the stuff that has been dominating your life for the last however many months. The first task is therefore to tell them all what it is about, rapidly and succinctly. Then go round the table and ask each of them why they think they're there and what difference they think they can make. Make it time limited and keep the pace up. If you have any external partners in the room, ensure they are deferred to and given appropriate air time, otherwise they will feel aggrieved and you will lose the bid.

At this point you will learn or realise that everyone thinks they know how to do or run great presentations. Very few people on planet Earth know how to do even mediocre presentations, but you are going to run great ones. So follow closely.

Be clear that you have the mandate to be in charge, you are inclusive, attentive to what others have to say, but diplomatic in disregarding their more insane remarks. Rehearse carefully with the team the kind of questions the client may ask and get the team to write them down and share them

Then decide in advance of learning any precise detail from the client what the presentation of your overall proposition will look like. Start with the people you will have on parade. One of the greatest coaches and sages in presentation training advised that the bid director should open the presentation by presenting the team individually, highlighting their specialisms and the key roles they will have on the project or in the relationship with the client. "This is Elvis Houston, he is CEO of Chandelier Enterprises. Through him we are accountable to the main board for the performance of this contract. Before being CEO at Chandelier Enterprises, Elvis was chief operating officer at Pratt and Pratt, where he re-engineered the business and improved client satisfaction by 1,000%...."

"This is Dave Donothing, he will be the programme manager, responsible for delivery. You will hear from Dave every day and he will be a key member of the steering group..."

This way, we avoid mumbling, boring, self-introductions and the client gets a solid picture of who's who in the zoo. Opinions vary on presenting the proposition. Does one person – the solution owner – do this, or do you break it up. Depending on the time available, better to break it up. Get the specialists talking about the solution or offer, but manage the time really carefully. Talking too much and too long is a real turnoff for the listener – because the client will want to ask questions at some point. Some clients will even have stopwatches to ensure fairness between bidders.

Next is the need to tackle the "why should I bother to give you this job?" aspect of all sales pitches and presentations. The answer will always be a combination of cost, capability, quality of your people and whether they like you or not. All of this can be dressed up in the jargon of your particular industry, but be careful of too much management speak. Endless use of value chains, solution propositions and end-to end dynamics will ultimately bamboozle the client and make you sound like everyone else. You want to win; therefore you need to be clear, concise and insightful, giving the client reason to think that not only did these guys submit a great written bid, they have now taken us into the reality of delivery and how we are going to work together. How great is that!

Remember if a time slot is 20 minutes, 21 minutes is not acceptable; none of you are so special that you can run over time.

We now have to come out of the closet and address the supporting materials we will use. Inevitably this leads to PowerPoint, the lower point of all presentations and where the potential for value destruction is almost tangible. The first question to ask is, "do we really need it?" Not having it can act against you, so the follow up is should we project it on screen or just take hand-outs for the client? The latter may be sufficient without the big screen experience because it avoids the need to mess about with technology – yours or theirs – which can cause delay and stress when you least need it. It also allows the clients to engage more interactively with your story, because a good presentation needs a narrative. In general, listeners switch off when looking at big screens, so if you are using a big screen, remember that less is more and don't go for a 50 slide deck – a maximum of ten slides will always work – no matter what you are talking about. Don't overcrowd the slide with dinky little icons and images from the infinite PowerPoint palette – keep the messages clear and uncluttered. After all, you're not going to read them out. You should also give your audience time to absorb them, if you do not wish them to be regarded as electronic wallpaper.

Handing out a nice personalised document with a few pages and plenty of room for the client to doodle or make notes is far more effective and engaging and you can move them through it by the simple expedient of saying, "And now look at page 3."

There are times when a bespoke video may need to be shown, to illustrate some market research for example, or to show a particular process in action; if so you will need to read the sequel to this book "Bite-sized digital media" if and when it is produced. Suffice it to say that the same basic rules apply, keep it short and snappy and above all audible.

Once you have the skeleton of the text mapped out, you now need to rehearse roles and write the script – and I really mean rehearse. Participants need to write down what they are going to say, not with a view to reading it out (terrible), but with a view to learning it and timing the delivery. Delivery is an art; preparation is a science. And you are in charge. When all is set, you can go for one of many dummy runs in front of the wider squad who can pretend to be the client panel, not from the point of view of some kind of ludicrous "red team" inquisition, but from the perspective of knowing the requirement and being attentive to the best way of improving the understanding of the offer through the medium of the presentation.

Senior people hate this, as do other experts who reckon they know how to do great presentations – of course they don't unless they've read this Bite-Sized Book and have taken their daily humility pills. Your critical friends can then give unvarnished feedback on performance.

If we fast forward to the actual day of the formal presentation itself, you should ensure that you are able to get the team together the day before if the presentation is the following morning, or in the morning if it is in the afternoon for a final run through and time check; this time with only the team doing the presentation

The essential message of this chapter and the reason for its title is that you should not start with the PowerPoint, you should start with the conversation from which the presentation materials should fall out. It is too easy to put slides together without the thought of the narrative that should inform them and crucially without building and rehearsing the team effectively to deliver the story. Do it this way and you will not allow technology and ego to destroy value.

Chapter 6
Buying Signals: Meet the Procurement Professionals

OK, so this book is all about bidding, big and small. A key point to remember is that buyers increasingly have been to procurement school. Procurement, purchasing, buying, sourcing – often with the word global as a prefix, is now a science. You can take diplomas and degrees in it and join professional bodies that issue codes of best practice and admit you to a procurement club.

Global organisations such as the WTO negotiate trade agreements, the EU issues directives, EFTA haggles on the side lines, APEC stitches up Asia Pacific at multilateral levels and all this percolates down to rules and regulations in different territories, interpreted to the letter in the UK or not at all if we're in Italy or Indonesia. In both public and private sectors, procurement departments are well established, their members attend international conferences where they discuss the value chain, global sourcing, outsourcing, insourcing, upsourcing, downsourcing, singlesourcing, multiplesourcing, on-line sourcing roundaboutsourcing and so it goes on.

All of this has to be borne in mind, by you the bite-sized bidder, looking to win some honest work, often to be purchased with public money that you have contributed towards through your taxes.

So let's take a look at public and private sectors and throw in some not-for-profits as well. Bearing in mind that whilst the purpose of being bite-sized is not to put you off, you do need to understand what is increasingly common in all sectors and how best to spend your time. Big government procurement, for example for battleships and aircraft, requires big company bidding departments able to operate internationally for deals that last for decades and where the winner takes all.

It is these kinds of procurements that have driven the rules and regulations about competition, conflicts of interest, national interest versus free trade, monopolies and mergers, oligopolies and privileged trading rights. All this stuff ultimately impacts on the little guys, be they part of the supply chain for large enterprises or whether they are bidding for lower value business.

So how do you seek out, find or otherwise recognise buying signals from potential clients who may want to spend serious dosh with your business by way of some kind of formal procedure?

Well, you need to set out who you are and what you are selling and most importantly why you are special, different (avoid being unique – chances are you won't be) distinctive and reliable. You have to answer the buying signallers' endless question, "Why should I bother buying from you?" or more bluntly, "Why should I even bother talking to you?"

Remember, you will encounter varying degrees of arrogance from the buyers because they have the money – and you don't. Unfortunately, the advent of email and on-line buying has made it more difficult to engage with procurement professionals – and believe me they like it that way. Phone numbers are now more difficult to obtain and the standard position is to make the process more anodyne and apparently equal through e-procurements.

You need a brief descriptor of your offer – the so-called elevator pitch. You need to be clear about who you are and your ideas, skills and reputation. You also will need to show financial worthiness. If you have some accounts to show, you will need them. If not, letters from banks or guarantees from malleable relatives for small scale opportunities may suffice (although don't try this if you are thinking of punting for some major defence contracts).

After capability and financial worthiness comes reliability. Where have you sold your stuff before? Do you have other customers who like it? Do you have a website that oozes competence and track record? Is it up to date with cool pictures of yourself and your team? What does your CV look like – no need to mention that you were in the boy-scouts, although the younger you are the more achievements you should acknowledge.

Find out if the organisations to which you want to sell have open days or webinars for suppliers and attend them religiously. Ask intelligent questions. Always say who you are and what you or your company does, clearly and concisely. Get yourself recognised. Remember you are a specialist in what you do. Procurement professionals are specialists as well and they like to be recognised, because unlike, say medicine, procurement is a relatively new science, and status and standing are important for often fragile egos.

Once capability is established, you need to check out the specific opportunities. It they are services or products that are required, you will need to express interest, via an EOI (expression of interest). This may lead to something called a PQQ (pre-qualification questionnaire), which if passed, will lead to an RFP (Request for proposal) or an ITT (invitation to tender) or and ITN (invitation to negotiate) or whatever the voguish acronym is at the time. Remember, procurement is a science these days and therefore terminology is changing all the time as new frontiers are discovered.

You get through the EOI and PQQ or comparable stages and buying signals will be flashing a kind of green colour, alas not just for you but also for our competitors. You could easily be one of four, six or eight or even ten. You may even be just making up the numbers, but let's hope not. What happens next? An actual RFP. This is big stuff because it is time consuming and from the beginning you need to prepare for what may be the end. You need to appraise really carefully, whether you should proceed at this point. Now, the buyers will tell you that if you have passed all the preliminaries successfully and then you don't bid, you will ruin your reputation and they won't bother with you ever again. This is because a critical success factor for procurement professionals is having sufficient quantity of competent bidders.

Their worst outcome is a no-bid situation, or bidders withdrawing. So their buying signals may just possibly a tad deceptive and in all the bumph that you sign up to there is a common phrase along the lines of the buyer can halt the process at any time and that's just tough. However, if you withdraw, that is bad news. What I would say, if, as the process proceeds, it is not looking good for you commercially, stand by your principles and withdraw gracefully explaining carefully the reasons why. You should then copy that withdrawal to the CEO or most senior figure in the buying organisation, or write to them separately. Buyers won't like this, but you will retain your self-respect and also alert senior people to what the underlings are up to – as they don't always know and therefore need to be told.

Anyway, let's hope your RFP submission is successful and you get invited to negotiate with your client, or even better they just buy straightaway – this rarely happens. For services, a presentation meeting, or may be several will be essential (see earlier chapters on how to survive and thrive).

At this point you may be required for some post tender negotiations if you are what is known as a preferred bidder, this essentially means that the buyer is seeking a price reduction, or as they will put it, greater value for money. Make no mistake the words economically advantageous, mean, "how much cheaper can we get the deal?" You can offer additional services if you like, but what they want is a lower price and what you want is to do a great job and make money and to establish a productive relationship with the buyer.

Ensuring the buyer understands that you have to make money is important and you should be prepared to reveal what percentage that is. Obfuscation on costs and profits is not a good foundation for a commercial relationship with suppliers or with markets as Tesco in the UK has recently discovered. Better to be transparent rather than opaque.

Increasingly, we all want to know more about what we purchase and the ethical dimension to procurement is part of the process or integrity testing.

You should make every effort to meet the buyers and the specialists in the purchasing organisation and to understand what they want and how you can meet or exceed that need. Breaking in to a new big client is not easy but neither is it impossible. Whilst you may have no friends in competitive bidding or competitive tendering, you will have some allies whom you should cultivate and in whom you should invest in relationship development. People do buy people and if you are reasonable, flexible, clear and honest with a genuinely necessary or desirable product or service, you will be a successful bite-sized bidder.

The most successful people all share an ability to focus on what really matters, keeping things understandable and simple. MBAs, metrics and methodologies have their place, but when we are faced with a new business challenge most of us need quick guidance on what matters most, from people who have been there before and who can show us where to start. As Stephen Covey famously said, "The main thing is to keep the main thing, the main thing".

But what exactly is the main thing?

We created Bite-Sized books to help answer precisely that question crisply and quickly, working with writers who are experienced, successful and, of course, engaging to read.

The brief? Distil the *main things* into a book that can be read by an intelligent non-expert comfortably in around 60 minutes. Make sure the book provides the reader with specific tools, ideas and plenty of examples drawn from real life and business. Be a virtual mentor.

Bite-Sized Books don't cover every eventuality, but they are written from the heart by successful people who are happy to share their experience with you and give you the benefit of their success.

25687279R00020

Printed in Poland
by Amazon Fulfillment
Poland Sp. z o.o., Wrocław